90-Seconds To A Great

Relationship

90-Seconds To A Great Relationship

The Power of the *90-Second Rule™*

By Jim Fannin

"The World's #1 Coach of Champions"

This book is dedicated to
the "love of my life" and my awesome wife, CeCe.
I love you more than all the stars in the sky and
sand on the beach.
You inspire me every day

TABLE OF CONTENTS

INTRODUCTION

My name is Jim Fannin. I coach champions. For over 40-years, I've helped the world's best male and female athletes and executives become the best they can be. Although a bona fide champion is rare, there is someone that is even more rare. This is the true champion. The true champion is definitely great in their field of expertise. I've coached men and women champions from 10 major professional sports and executives from over 50 industries. However, true champions are more than their careers. The true champion is a great spouse or significant other, parent, sibling, son or daughter and friend. Also, they are at their best with their own money, spirituality and wellbeing.

What do most people need? I've discovered it's a more dynamic and loving personal relationship. For decades I've fielded phone calls 24/7 from 4am in the morning to 11pm at night. The biggest challenge for most of my clients is NOT their career but balancing it with their personal life. They all strive to maintain a positive, loving long-term relationship. The relationship tools you will find in this book have been time-tested and proven for over four decades. Your nationality, religious affiliation, age, or experience doesn't matter. The 90-Seconds to a Great Relationship techniques that will be revealed to you are powerful, swift and they work! Enjoy the contents. Take these tools and build or rebuild your most successful relationship possible.

Jim

WHAT DO YOU WANT IN YOUR RELATIONSHIP?

You have spent considerable time, money, effort, and emotion in your "significant other" relationship. I'm sure you'd like a positive return on this long-term investment. How's it going? Have you begun to settle? Has the relationship dynamic withered? Are both of your minds on careers, children and other challenges? Is it time to rekindle the passion? Is it time to guarantee the "forever" bond? Are you ready to take your relationship to a higher level? If the answer to any of these questions is YES, then it's time to install the power of the 90-Second Rule™.

Here's the end game most relationships desire. You and your significant other have a shared vision regarding your future. You both wake up happy and go to bed happy every day. No more quarrels. No bickering, silly disputes or arguments. Meanness has transformed into kindness. Silence is a harmonious and peaceful pleasure and not a punishment. In fact, love has taken over the relationship and catapulted the romance to a mature, intimate place. Small details of discontent are tabled or forgotten. The victim and judge in both of you have left the relationship for good. Your house has blossomed into a loving and content home. You are finishing each other's thoughts in a good way. You are happy meeting life's challenges together. You are respectful to each other. She or he stops in mid-sentence to let you finish the punch line of a story being told in front of friends. Intimacy has been elevated. Spontaneity is an every day occurrence. Touching has replaced avoidance. You hold hands for no reason. You snuggle watching a movie. You make each other laugh and you make each other better people. Your relationship is in a "purposeful calm" Zone. You look forward to being in each other's presence when you're apart. One plus one equals more than two. You are more together as a couple than apart. Your true best friend has arrived and it's mutual. Life's journey is thoroughly enjoyed as a couple. Life is more than good. Life as a loving couple is awesome!

What if only a few 90-second investments per day could guarantee more happiness, connectivity, and passion in your relationship? What if this investment could magically turn your relationship into the one that I just described. That's an investment of less than one percent (1%) of your daily, waking hours.

Are you ready? It's possible and it's awesome!

THE GREAT RELATIONSHIP MINDSET

The average person has between 2,000 and 3,000 thoughts every day. That's 4,000 to 6,000 collective thoughts for the average couple! No wonder life can become complicated. These thoughts are either positive or negative. It is one or the other. However, you could be positive and your partner could be negative or vice versa. You cannot individually hold a positive and negative thought simultaneously. Daily thoughts can be catalogued as future, past or present. Likewise, you cannot hold a future or past thought at the same time.

The busier your life becomes, the more thoughts you have. The positives and the negatives of your job, work or career typically take over your thoughts like weeds overrunning a garden. You are the gardener. You must provide the water and sunshine nourishment for your mind. You must till the soil and plant positive seeds of harmony. Unfortunately, many people wake up and see their mental garden overrun with the weeds of discontent and unhappiness especially in their "significant other" life arena.

"Change your thoughts and your relationship will change."

Every thought you have is an electrical current that can be measured on a machine in the hospital called an encephalograph. Each thought, therefore, is an action. We know that with every action there is a reaction. However, a single thought has three simultaneous reactions all controlled by your subconscious mind. These reactions are physical, emotional and intuitive. They are readily readable. Bad thoughts produce negative physical reactions such as rolling your eyes, blowing your breath or frowning. Good thoughts for example produce smiles, positive head nods or bright eyes. Every thought also triggers a chemical response, which produces various feelings of sadness, happiness, envy, jealousy and etc. Happy thoughts trigger endorphins to flow into your blood stream and you feel happy. Likewise, you can feel the negative emotions created from your negative thoughts. Lastly, your thoughts send out positive or negative vibes that is picked up through intuition regardless of your geographical distance. Yikes! Here's what's important — You need to think about what you think about. Every thought is being broadcast. In order to upgrade your relationship, thoughts from you and your significant other must be upgraded.

"Think about what you think about."

When you first began dating your partner, your daily thoughts were flooded with positivity about the future Mr. or Mrs. Right. Your positive thoughts were showcased physically with your body language, emotionally with how you felt, and intuitively with how you broadcasted your thoughts.

Yes, all of your thoughts are being broadcast. That is the good news. Now of course, that could be the bad news and this is where 90-Seconds to a Great Relationship becomes an insurance policy for keeping all of your thoughts positive.

*"Good thoughts float at the top with hope.
Negative thoughts sink to the bottom with despair."*

By selecting this book with its title and reading its content, I know you want more in your relationship than what you have right now. Before we begin, make sure you are committed to this major upgrade in your relationship. Starve the victim in you. Remove the judge. By feeding good thoughts to the True Champion in you, positive changes <u>will</u> occur.

<u>You</u> must be the first to change. Make up your mind that you are going to a better place even if your partner chooses not to. This you can control. Your thoughts can and will influence your partner in a powerful way. Vow to no longer put your "significant other" down in your mind, in front of him or her or to friends. Vow to possess relationship self-discipline. Vow to be the best "significant other" and the best person you can be. Then get ready for great things to happen because they will!

Great Relationships Need Self-Discipline

This is the willingness and commitment to stay with positive daily routines that lead to well-defined relationship goals that take you to a shared vision with the one you love.

THE POWER OF THE 90-SECOND RULE™

**It takes less than 90-seconds to change your mind
and positively reverse your course of action.**

Throughout my coaching career I've realized that the best in the world make swift decisions to right a sinking ship or alter their course for immediate positive change. And the best can do this in less than 90-seconds. Why not you? This crucial decision making ability was applied to setting positive routines for preparation, adjustment and evaluation. For over four decades this was the successful model for my coaching.

There are five daily usages of the 90-Second Rule™ that form the **90-Seconds to a Great Relationship.** This guarantees a dynamic, loving relationship. They are:

- 90-Second Rule™ (Good Morning)
- 90-Second Rule™ (Good-bye)
- 90-Second Rule™ (Mental Movie)
- 90-Second Rule™ (Greeting)
- 90-Second Rule™ (Good Night)

Let's get started!

The 90-Second Good Morning

Selfishness has no part of this 1st powerful tool. It sets the tone for the entire day. Get off to a great start and it will be clear sailing. Wake up selfish, grumpy and in a bad mood...well, you know the answer.

When you just awake from a night's sleep, open your eyes and find your significant other. This must be prepared for the night before. Positive energy occurred in the morning when you awoke the first time you spent the night together. Complacency over time typically takes over. Individualism permeates one or both partners. Taking the morning for granted does not have a place here. Selfishness leads to loneliness. Know this, if you do not already.

"Wake up happy and happy will follow you all day."

Devote the first 90-seconds of your day to your mate, spouse or significant other. Your devotion might find him or her under the covers with you, in the bathroom or in the kitchen. It's also possible that you do not physically awake with this person. Find them with your thoughts and find them physically, if possible. Then:

- Tell them you love them.
- Tell them it's a great day to be with them.
- Smile.
- Hug.
- Kiss.
- It's NOT about you. Be positive. No grumpiness.
- No complaining. No approaching the day with dread. Send the positivity even if it is only for the initial 90-seconds.
- Set the tone. Make the out loud declaration (unless they're fast asleep) that "It's an awesome day!", or "It's a great day to be with you", or "I'm the luckiest person in the world! That's because I'm with you."
- If your partner is asleep, whisper with your lowest voice, "I love you" or another familiar "sweet nothing." Stroke their hair. Rub their arm gently.

My partner took this to another level. I DO NOT recommend this. She tweezed my eyebrows while I was sleeping! I kept waking up and looked over and she faked being asleep. I thought a bug or mosquito bit me. God love her. She actually thought she was performing a loving act. But I did finally catch her in the act.

- If a quick goodbye needs to occur, say goodbye like you mean it. If possible, look them in the eye long enough to discern eye color. Send your "significant other" into their day with good intentions, positivity and great energy. Let's focus a bit more on this most critical part of your day.

"A whispered 'I love you' is very loud and clear."

The 90-Second Good-bye

This is the best good-bye you'll ever experience. Make it so.

"The words of your good-bye last longer when delivered with your eyes."

Most mornings, families and couples around the country are doing the same thing. They are rushing and hurrying. They are frantically getting dressed for work to avoid the morning rush hour. They are preparing breakfast for their children before school. Screamed directives are flying throughout the house as everyone in the household has their own hurried agenda. The mood is grumpy at best for many families. Conversations are few and goodbyes are short and often neglected entirely. Is this happening in your house?

Always carve out 90-seconds for a meaningful good-bye. Look your significant other in the eye long enough to discern eye color and tell him or her that you love them and will miss them. Within this brief minute and a half, you set the future for when you will speak or be with them again. Embrace. Hug like you mean it. Smell their hair, clothes, cologne or perfume. Carve this special time to be alone (even in a crowd) with the one you love. Taking good-byes for granted has haunted many people. Say good-bye with all your love and devotion oozing from every pore. Be sure to make this brief farewell meaningful. It sets the tone for everything else.

The 90-Second Mental Movie

All of your thoughts portray images or pictures. Many of these thoughts are in mini-movies complete with visuals, sound, smell, taste and feel. Most people think and consequently see what they **DON'T** want in their lives as opposed to what they **DO** want. If your relationship is not clicking on all cylinders, it's easy to envision or play the mini-movie of what you **DON'T** want. One of you in the relationship must flip the script on the content and quality of both the individual and collective thoughts of the partnership. Remember: your relationship is only as good as what your partner thinks when you're not there. <u>YOU</u> need to start the ball rolling!

"Shared vision brought you together:
Shared vision will keep you together."

At least twice daily, carve out 90-seconds to envision the love of your life. Remember when you were dating? Your mind was possessed with the images, smells and sounds of the other person in your life. Let's rekindle some of these images on a regular basis. Some years ago I was coaching a professional heavyweight fighter and I introduced to him the power of positive visualization. He swiftly told me he had never done this before. Then I asked him to tell me about his fiancé. He broke into a huge grin as he described how she looked. He could see in his mind's eye every detail of her. He even attempted to describe the smell of her perfume. When I stopped him and made him aware that he was already an expert at visualization, you should have seen the look on his face! Immediately we started incorporating visualization into his profession. It works.

"The power of visualization is to never have a day that
you haven't already had."

Let me clarify. Break away from the daily grind of what you do. Give focused energy in seeing and feeling happiness, laughter, confidence, tranquility, and passion radiating from your partner. Twice per day while apart and within 90-seconds or less, do the following:

- Mentally picture him or her happy.
- See them being successful.
- See them in a fun and exciting manner.
- See them overcoming their challenges in a completed state.
- See their loving, smiling face.
- See and feel their warm embrace.
- Taste their kisses. (There are no rules here!)
- Visualize as if it's so.
- See she or he, as they will be.

Your significant other will eventually pick up on your positive vibe. They will be able to tell that there is a major difference in the air. Keep the positivity flowing on a regular basis and the results will arrive.

The 90-Second Greeting
(after you've been apart at least 2-hours)

This usage of the *90-Second Rule*™ has played with great success in Australia, China, Peru, Italy, Spain, England, France, Germany,

Austria, Sweden, Ireland, Canada, South Africa and the United States. It is truly universal in its appeal and successful application. This 90-seconds is crucial! It was my mother's favorite. Your partner will immediately notice a difference. In fact, the reaction from your partner and family will be very interesting. Here are some typical responses from significant others around the globe. "What's up with you?" "Are you okay?" "So...what have you done?" "Who told you to do this?"

Ready? Make this a definite daily routine. My guess is that you'll never go home the same again. If you've been away from someone you care about and love for at least two hours, the first 90-seconds you see them has more impact on your relationship than spending hours and hours with them later. Do the following:

- Put away your cell phone. Make the last call in the driveway. Send that last text.
- Clear your mind from what transpired in your life prior to this moment.
- Immediately upon walking through the door, find your "significant other." Look him or her in the eye long enough to discern eye color (you'll probably discover that you have not been doing this).
- If you have children, hold them up so you can hug Mommy or Daddy first. Now you are showing your children how to treat a "significant other." And you are showing respect to your life partner.
- Use the "mirroring" technique. If your life partner is sad, then mirror their sadness (not for you to be sad) but so you can connect swiftly with their feelings. Show instant empathy. Then within a few seconds, bring them up to a higher level of positivity. Mentally walk them into a positive future if that is appropriate. If they are happy and excited, then reflect this enthusiasm and act happy and excited. Mirroring goes a long way to establishing a great evening and night.
- Hug them. Kiss them. Give these abundantly. This is not the obligatory, courtesy hug or peck on the cheek. Mean it!

This usage of the 90-Second Rule™ says...

- I love you.
- I missed you.
- I value you.
- I need you in my life.

Yes. This 90-seconds is designed for relationships but it is not limited to couples alone. Long-time client and former Major League Baseball player Jose Cruz, Jr. has been utilizing this usage of the 90-Second Rule™ for a decade. In fact, his awesome wife and three children are also using this powerful tool when they come home from being apart for at least two hours.

"'I Believe in You' is a Statement that Builds Relationships"

In addition, Mrs. Denise Fitzgerald, a third grade teacher at a public school in Chicago, has introduced my S.C.O.R.E.® Success System with its toolbox of 90-Second Rule™ tools to her classes. Every morning, she greets each student by looking them in the eye long enough to discern eye color. The 90-Second Rule™ is in her classroom. She showers each student with radiating positivity. In turn, each student greets their classmates by doing the same. Her classroom of "official" Zoniacs™ is a collection of peak performers. Not only have their grades increased, but their social awareness and overall attitude has soared. What a bright future they will have!

The 90-Second Good Night

If you get and apply one thing from this book, PLEASE get this next use of the 90-Second Rule™. This is a big-time game changer for relationships. It just might be the single biggest difference maker in whether a relationship has success or failure. Allow me to explain. It all has to do with how the human brain functions.

There are two times in a 24-hour cycle when your subconscious mind naturally is amenable to suggestion. They are 30-minutes before you sleep and 30-minutes after you awake. Every thought you have during these times will be replayed 15-20 times while in a deep sleep. Now you know why you have sleepless nights.

Like fertile soil, your subconscious mind will readily receive good seeds and/ or bad seeds during these times. When the seeds of discontentment, unhappiness, jealousy, frustration or lack of trust are planted night after night and morning after morning, they will grow into their physical equivalent. By thinking about the possibility of separating because of this negativity for 7-10 consecutive days, your subconscious mind will figure out a way to make it so. These seeds of separation or divorce can be planted without your conscious knowledge. Anger, animosity, hatred, loneliness and despair will arrive with negative actions governing your waking hours. Conversely, when the seeds of love, trust, harmony, peace and passion are planted, your relationship will grow into a redwood of unity, prosperity and everlasting love.

Make the following agreement with your partner (if possible) before either of you drift off into the REM state of deep sleep. The last 30-minutes of your day are devoted exclusively to thinking positive and the last 90-seconds are devoted entirely to the two of you. This routine is about giving, sharing, loving and nurturing. Peaceful, loving silence is totally acceptable.

If a disagreement cannot be resolved before the day ends and you are at an impasse, agree to resolve your differences the next day. However, the 90-Second Rule™ before deep sleep still applies. No matter what transpired before sleep, DO NOT, I repeat DO NOT allow the negative to go to sleep with you. Period!

Dwell on Positive Outcomes and Negative Consequences Go Away

During the last 30-minutes and especially within the last 90-seconds of being awake follow these guidelines:

* ★ Always talk in low-pitched tones.
* ★ Talk slow . . . . . and calm . . . . Whispers rock!
* ★ Focus on one another in the present tense.
* ★ Be honest without opening up a circumstance, condition or situation that cannot be resolved before sleep.
* ★ DO NOT bring up other life arenas such as finances, children, job or personal health.
* ★ Avoid ALL talk about the past. It's not the time.
* ★ Genuinely care about what the other feels, not just thinks. See through their eyes and feel through their feelings. Understand that compassion spawns passion.
* ★ Eliminate all judgment thoughts.

* Eliminate all victim thoughts.
* Talk only about the future in a positive, solution oriented and loving way. Only your shared vision thoughts as a couple are acceptable.
* Compliment.
* Deal from your relationship strengths.
* Be silent in harmony and solidarity. You'll feel it.
* Hold hands, hug, cuddle, kiss, rub toes, or caress.
* Close the night with statements of "I love you," "I believe in you," "I appreciate you" or other loving, caring "I" statements.
* Yes...this usage of the 90-Second Rule™ occurs AFTER intimacy!

"Mom was right! Go to bed happy."

Of the hundreds of marriages I've personally helped reconnect to a higher level, this tool has played a major role. Visualization rocks within the last 30-minutes before sleep and will benefit you and your relationship on a multitude of levels.

Be Yourself!
You're the only one in the world that can do that.

COUPLES FIRST AID KIT

There are *only* five uses of the 90-Second Rule™ that make up the **90-Seconds to a Great Relationship.** I told a good friend of mine about how he could change his relationship with his spouse in only nine minutes. He was so excited to learn that this was even possible. Of course, he was bummed when he realized that it was an investment of 9 minutes EVERY day (90-seconds at a time). He had hoped it was only 9 minutes once and forever. His marriage could be in trouble, don't you think?

You may need more 90-Second Rule™ tools to combat a myriad of unexpected events, occurrences, circumstances, situations and conditions. Preparation is the key to handling any adverse time. Here is a short list of simple, proven tools to get you and your relationship back in the Zone — the Zone of the True Champion. Choose wisely from this section because every relationship is different.

"Keep your chin up especially when your burdens weigh the most."

Life can get complicated. You can easily get ambushed with a myriad of challenges in a short amount of time. Below are some 90-Second Rule™ tools that have been time tested for handling a crisis or adverse situation, condition or circumstance. Other tools in the Couples First Aid Kit section are bonus tools for adding more pizazz in your relationship. Choose the ones that are appropriate for you and arm yourself for the unexpected. It's going to happen.

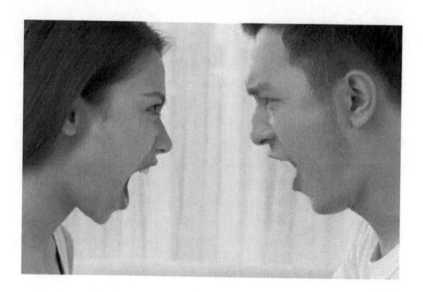

THE PALM TREE™

Your thoughts, feelings and actions happen daily. Are you aware of them? There are many body language mannerisms that you perform that you are not consciously aware of. There are feelings of frustration, jealousy, embarrassment that can occur without your acknowledgement. This can lead to arguments, disagreements and even silent anger with your mate or spouse. This Palm Tree™ tool may be just the technique that makes life more simple and easy.

The palm tree reacts to a hurricane or violent storm by allowing the negativity to pass through it by bending with the violent winds. IT absorbs the energy and the devastating wrath of the storm. After the hurricane dissipates and departs, the palm stands up straight to see another day of sunshine. It symbolizes all that's good about the sun, beach, ocean, recreation and pleasure.

An oak tree, of course, would brace itself and fight the 80 to 100 mph forces. It would fight with all of its strength to not succumb to the hurricane's fury. With a mighty, but futile attempt, it would be left with broken branches or tree trunk. Maybe it would be uprooted and scattered. This is why you never see oak trees on the beach. Hurricanes of life are more frequent than the real ones that wreak havoc on our beaches. They arrive internally and externally into our lives. Some we create and others are cast upon us.

Are you a palm tree or an oak tree in the face of adversity? Most of the time a Palm Tree™ attitude works and the demeanor of an oak tree does not. Although IF the situation presents itself you may need to stand tall like the mighty oak and say, "This is not acceptable."

Keep both the Palm Tree™ and oak tree images in your mind. Be armed when the time comes to wield their services. Be aware of your thoughts and feelings and you will control your actions and ultimately your results.

Managing any negative forces depends on how you think during situations, conditions and circumstances of stress. Here's how to manage the psychological hurricanes that arrive in your life. Within 90-Seconds of receiving negative news, having a major disagreement, reality not meeting your expectations, abuse from a road-raged driver, or being placed on hold by the utility company, become the palm tree by doing the following:

1. Unhinge your jaw
2. Lower your breathing to approximately 6 to 8 breaths per minute
3. Picture a palm tree in your mind.
4. Without silence, absorb the negativity and let it pass through you like the palm tree.
5. After the hurricane blows itself out, visualize the outcome you want.
6. Feel the sunshine on your face. Smile internally.
7. Regularly remind yourself of the Palm Tree™ tool.

Now you know the Palm Tree™ and you'll be ready when a life hurricane arrives. When the negative winds from situations, conditions or circumstances become apparent; you'll become relaxed, poised and peaceful. This will take practice and preparation, as life's "surprises" will certainly catch you off guard. In the next few days, be aware of your true thoughts and feelings. Try this method the next time you are in a situation that could lead to anger, especially if you are with your "significant other". As soon as a circumstance, condition or event displeases you or disturbs you, think of the palm tree. Immediately have a Palm Tree™ thought before the human hurricane reaches full force. You'll react like a True Champion!

"Be the Palm Tree in all of life's hurricanes."

BREATHE LIKE A BABY™

This technique is how little infants fall asleep so easily. It's also how your dog can be fetching a ball...then you get on your cellphone...and when you finally look for your dog, she or he is sleeping and maybe even snoring. Both the baby and dog relax by using this 90-Second Rule™ technique. That's right! It takes less than 90-seconds for it to take effect.

When your thoughts get thicker, your breaths get quicker. Slow both and you'll feel better and see more clearly.

When your under stress, your heart is pounding, breathing is difficult and you're definitely not in the Zone, try this:

Begin by inhaling deeply. Unhinge your jaw. Place all of your awareness on your breathing. Feel your lungs fill with positive, energized air. Now exhale negative air. Place your left or right hand on your stomach. With each inhale and exhale, allow your stomach to move your hand. Breathe through your stomach. Be aware of your hand being moved.

After a few deep breaths, you'll start to feel your shoulders relax. Slowly, repeat inhaling and exhaling, until you are in a relaxed rhythm. Within 30-90-Seconds you will feel more relaxed. Now send all of your energy away from you to a well-defined target or objective. You're ready to launch an energy flow. Use this technique anytime and anywhere.

"True champions just look cool.
You seldom see them sweat."

Remember: your supposed "nervousness" was just your body preparing to "Get in the Zone." Now you know what to do.

LOVE CONQUERS ALL

This blunt statement can resolve most relationship challenges. It is the bottom line for successful couples. "I don't like you right now," is a thought or statement that for the moment may be justified and true. "However, I still love you", is the thought or statement that needs to prevail, regardless of any challenges that couples face every day.

No one is perfect. And our small imperfections are a part of the whole of us. It's easy for some couples to look past small indiscretions and inadequacies. On the other hand, when small things that bother us are mentally repeated, they can turn into major challenges. "Love conquers all" can help prevent replaying your significant other's negatives. Be open-minded to acceptance and understanding in your relationship. Communicate your thoughts in a loving way. Be positive. Let the other person know that what they did or are doing is bothersome to you, but can be solved.

"Kindness is a great salve for most wounds."

When your chest tightens and negatives start gurgling like lava preparing to launch from a volcano, think, "Love conquers all." And it does.

THE 90-SECOND SURPRISE

My wife listened to Michael Jackson growing up as a child. She knew all of his dance moves and could lip-sync all of his songs. When he died she was definitely impacted like millions of other fans around the world. The following Christmas Santa placed a thick, rare, red book that weighed 38 pounds. It contained photos never seen before of The King of Pop. She was blown away. It was a total surprise. However, surprise does not need to cost significant money. Yes, it's the thought that counts.

Of the most memorable times in your life, surprises are the most memorable. These moments caught you off guard. You never saw it coming. It came out of the blue. It seemingly just happened. You were overwhelmed. You were taken by surprise. It created a great and lasting memory.

What can you do in 90-seconds or less to surprise your significant other? Some time ago I wrote a handwritten note to my wife and hid it in the freezer. It said, "It's cold in here but I'm still hot for you!" Several weeks later while I was on a business trip she found it tucked amongst the frozen food. Surprise! Of course, my teenage daughter is still rolling her eyes in disgust. But that's OK.

"Positive surprises will keep your relationship fresh."

Think out of the box. For most, the 90-Second Rule™ tools in this book will be a surprise to the one you love. Bring home his or her favorite dessert for no reason. Surprise. Make the bed especially if you've NEVER made the bed. Surprise. Buy a single rose. Surprise.

Bring breakfast in bed. Surprise. Draw him or her a bubble bath. Surprise. Give a foot rub with oil. Surprise. You get the message. Surprise!

THE 90-SECOND MAKE-OUT

Can you be intimate for only 90-seconds? Why not? My spouse occasionally has been upset with me about something I forgot to do. I know it's hard to believe. At the moment of her displeasure, I've blurted out with a deadpan demeanor, "I guess making out right now is out of the question." The first time I said this she was stymied to the point of breaking into laughter. She even forgot why she was upset with me. Use this tool judiciously.

"Passion is the fuel for togetherness."

Intimate moments woven into a busy day can be loving, caring and definitely nurturing. An intimate 90-seconds of caressing, kissing, hugging, embracing, petting, touching or fondling is something you've probably done before. Isn't it time to rekindle the flame? Don't you want to put down this book and get busy? 90-seconds is all it takes!

"Physical touch makes a difference."

THE 90-SECOND SMILE

Smile for 90-seconds in front of your significant other and there will be a response. "Why are you smiling?" "What are you up to?" "What's got into you?" "Have you lost your mind?" The odds are your mate or spouse will smile back. "I'm smiling because I realize how lucky I am to be with you" is a response they will never expect.

"Smile in the face of adversity and you'll find your way."

Smiles are contagious. You may need to practice. You definitely need to smile with some consistency. If your relationship has been void of smiles, then take the lead and start a smile-fest. Smile because life can be short. Smile because it feels good. Smile because that is one of the by-products of a great relationship. Smile because you love to see them smile.

MOOD MATTERS

How do you get your significant other in the mood? No...not that kind of mood. How do you get them in the positive "I love you" mood? Sometimes you might need to alter the mood by changing your environment. It could as simple as making small changes in your home. Adding music throughout the rooms definitely can change how a person thinks and feels. Choose music that reflects both of your tastes. When you first met, what was the popular music being played? It might be time to bring back the oldies but goodies. When I put on a Barry White CD, my wife gave me a wry smile and a look of "you've got to be kidding me." Of course, when I broke out into dance, I mentally whisked her far away from the daily grind of life and catapulted her into the moment. Try it. Your dance skill is irrelevant.

"Change how you feel by Changing how you think."

Fresh cut flowers or a new plant in a noticeable place are positive mood makers. Lowering the temperature or raising it can alter moods as well as increased or decreased lighting. Place a light behind a plant and the reflections might add just the touch needed to alter the mood. In fact, candles are definite mood makers. You know this. Now don't go candle crazy. Just add one scented candle in the bedroom and see what happens. Changing from an indoor to an outdoor environment can swiftly alter the mood. A candlelight dinner on an outdoor balcony could do the trick. Take a hand-held walk in the woods. Carve out a short weekend retreat.

What you wear can definitely change the mood. Loungewear, negligee, bathrobe and nothing at all could be major mood changers. Be appropriate. Be bold and daring. Be natural.

Yes! Mood matters.

THE RE-BOOT™

Sometimes you just need to wipe your mind clear. Over-thinking can be a hazard to your relationship health. Just like your personal computer, when your mental screen freezes, it has too many things on your mind or contains a warning, re-boot or turn it off. This solution is used to counter over-thinking as a reaction to a something you don't want.

"Free will gives you the power to always have a great day."

Here's how it works and it takes 90-seconds or less. Close your eyes. Slightly open your jaw. Visualize a clear or black screen in your mind's eye. Hold this black screen image for 90-seconds or less. You should have zero thoughts during the Re-Boot. As you open your eyes, hold your chin up above parallel. You should immediately smile or create a confident look of an "I can," or "I will" demeanor. Your mind is clear and ready to go. Do this at any time during your day when you feel the need to.

"Success is getting up one more time from defeat."

CONCLUSION

Before you were a committed couple, you had multiple, positive thoughts about the other person when you were apart. That's exactly what helped create the physical and mental connection. It's time to rekindle this positive imagery. And when you were with him or her, they could do nothing wrong. No little idiosyncrasies ever got in the way of your relationship. You were more tolerant. You were more empathetic. You were more forgiving and understanding. It's time to Re-Boot™ your overall relationship mindset and start anew.

"A single thought can reverse the outcome of any situation, condition or circumstance."

Life got more complicated from the time you met your "significant other" until now. It happens. When there are duel careers, children (especially teenagers), in-laws, step-kids, blended families, financial woes and/ or physical health challenges, it's easy to flood your mind with negativity. This is normal. This is happening all over the world. There is nothing wrong with you. Many times, a small adjustment and re-tooling is all you and your relationship needs. Make this an ongoing process and there will never again be the need for any major adjustments. Make a daily investment in your relationship by utilizing these 90-Second Rule™ tools. You can do this! This is a small investment that guarantees an incredibly large return.

Make these tools part of your daily routine. Envision your "significant other" smiling. Commit to a shared vision. You may need to make some sacrifices. You may need to make some personal adjustments. I'm certain these 90-second investments will produce the relationship you desire and the relationship you deserve.

"Talk up, never down."

Take a moment, shut your eyes and see your "significant other" equally committed to a more positive relationship. See your rejuvenated partnership, as it will be. With only a small investment each day, I know you can be more together than apart.

Spring into action. Start enjoying your amazing life...90-seconds at a time.

Good fortune favors the bold!

Jim

Fanninisms™

What follows is a small bonus collection of Jim Fannin relationship quotes from his many speeches, seminars, writings, and coaching sessions. Select the ones that fit your situation, condition and circumstance.

- *"If your heart's not in it, your eyes will quickly reveal the truth."*
- *"Dwell on positive outcomes and negative consequences go away."*
- *"A helping heart is greater than a helping hand."*
- *"Good thoughts float at the top with hope while negative thoughts sink to the bottom with despair."*
- *"Physical touch makes a difference."*
- *"A single thought can reverse the outcome of any situation, condition or circumstance."*
- *"You'll never heal until you stop thinking you're hurt."*
- *"What's said about you when you're not there is created by you."*
- *"You and your significant other together should equal more than apart or what's the point?"*
- *"Talk up, never down."*
- *"Committed love acknowledges the risk of vulnerability for both partners with trust negating the risk."*
- *"Sacrifice your personal wants and desires for the good of the whole."*
- *"Avoid speaking over your partner in public. Share the spotlight."*
- *"Old fashion values still work today. Hold the door open for her. Let the man open the door. If you have children, they're watching."*
- *"A whispered 'I love you' is very loud and clear."*

MORE FANNINISMS™

- *"If two partners always agree, then one is not needed."*
- *"Every relationship needs individual 'alone time'."*
- *"Avoid replaying the past unless it's for a good belly laugh."*
- *"Negative feelings left unexpressed eventually turn into negative actions."*
- *"Wrap your ego in a blanket of love and unity."*
- *"Whisper if you want to be heard."*
- *"Shared vision brought you together. Shared vision will keep you together."*
- *"Laughter helps mend most broken hearts."*
- *"'I believe in you' is a statement that builds relationships."*
- *"Yelling always muffles the essence of your message."*
- *"Relationships are partnerships built on trust."*
- *"Forgive quickly. Forgive often."*
- *"Have solidarity before going out in public together."*
- *"'I appreciate...' Use this judiciously, but use it."*
- *"Kindness is a great salve for most wounds."*
- *"Asking positive questions that can't be answered with yes or no will stimulate a positive dialogue."*
- *"Hold my hand and I'll feel secure. Hug me and I'll feel safe. Hug me tightly and I'll feel loved."*
- *"At an impasse, feel what they feel, see what they see, hear what they hear, and think what they think. Then use your intuition before your next move."*
- *"Dreams are personal. Support them."*
- *"Great couples make each other better."*

About Jim Fannin

Jim Fannin is the "World's #1 Coach of Champions" by producing more champions in life, business and sports than anyone on earth since 1974. He is a mental performance coach, author, professional platform speaker, life strategist, sports & business consultant, and former professional tennis player. He has 40+ years of professional coaching, consulting and public speaking experience.

Mr. Fannin has privately coached hundreds of professional athletes from 10 sports with 26 MLB All-Stars (including 4 Cy Young Award winners, 6 MVPs and two batting champions), Olympic gold medalists, seven world's top 10 ranked professional tennis players (including a 4-time Wimbledon Doubles Champion, French Open Champion and Runner-up), NBA All-Stars, NFL All-Pros, MLS MVP and 10 golfers to win their first professional tournament.

In addition, Jim has personally trained tens of thousands of corporate executives and hundreds of companies from 50 industries in peak performance. From leadership teams and sales organizations, Jim's thought management systems have made an impact.

With proprietary research on intuition, visualization and self-awareness, Jim customized his *S.C.O.R.E.® Success System* with its proven *90-Second Rule*™ tools and techniques for the world's elite athletes, top executives, business owners, couples, parents and students.

As one of world's foremost thought leaders, he is more than a life, business or sports coach. He is a "change your life" coach. With the ONLY proven blueprint for attracting the Zone mindset, he has helped transform millions of people's lives, providing them with simplicity, balance, and abundance.

Thousands of couples have used Jim's *90-Second Rule*™ tools and techniques to enhance and even save their relationships and marriages. Today there are more happy couples because of these simple, proven solutions for relationship challenges.

Jim and his wife live happily in the suburbs of Chicago, IL

THE JIM FANNIN EXPERIENCE

Join the ranks of some of the most successful people in the world by learning Jim's tools and techniques for all facets of your life, business and sport.

Get the "truth" about peak performance and life mastery from the world's #1 coach of champions, Jim Fannin. Over his 43-year amazing career, Jim has customized his patented *S.C.O.R.E.®* *Success System* with its *90-Second Rule*™ tools and techniques for tens of thousands of clients. All have been successful with most crushing personal, team and world records. Now Jim wants to help you

Start Now!

To experience the wisdom, knowledge, experience, insight and passionate energy from one of the world's foremost thought leaders, book Jim Fannin for:

Speaking engagements
Seminars
Executive coaching
Themed Retreats

Personal athlete coaching
Life coaching

If you enjoyed 90-Seconds to a Great Relationship™,
You'll love Jim's 90-Second Rule™ program.

Go to 90secondrule.com

For more information about Jim or to learn more about incorporating *90-Seconds to a Great Relationship*™ into your life or your next
event, visit www.jimfannin.com, call 877-210-2001 or email askjim@
jimfannin.com.

Also, be sure and follow Jim on:

Made in the USA
San Bernardino, CA
13 July 2015